REAL-LIFE
DRAGONS

EDGE

KOMODO
DRAGONS

by Jill Sherman

Consultant:
Colin Donihue, PhD
Postdoctoral Researcher
Department of Organismic and Evolutionary Biology
Harvard University
Cambridge, Massachusetts

CAPSTONE PRESS
a capstone imprint

Edge Books are published by Capstone Press,
1710 Roe Crest Drive, North Mankato, Minnesota 56003
www.mycapstone.com

Library of Congress Cataloging-in-Publication Data
Cataloging-in-Publication Data is available from the Library of Congress website.
ISBN 978-1-5157-5069-7 (library binding)
ISBN 978-1-5157-5073-4 (paperback)
ISBN 978-1-5157-5085-7 (eBook PDF)
Summary: Discusses the behavior, habitat, and life cycle of Komodo dragons.

Editorial Credits
Abby Colich, editor; Bobbie Nuytten, designer; Pam Mitsakos, media researcher;
Steve Walker, production specialist

Photo Credits
Getty Images: Joel Sartore, 27; iStockphoto: Frank Leung, 21; Minden Pictures:
Michael Pitts/NPL, 22, 23, Mike Lane/Biosphoto, 20, Nicolas Cegalerba/
Biosphoto, 24-25, Tui De Roy, 11; Newscom: Sijori Images/ZUMAPRESS.
com, 18; Shutterstock: Aleksandar Mijatovic, 8, Bob Orsillo, 5, Eric Isselee,
28, Erni, 4, Ethan Daniels, 26, GUDKOV ANDREY, 7, 12-13, kubais, 14,
reptiles4all, 9, Sergey Uryadnikov, cover bottom middle,   10, 17, Tor Pur, 16;
SuperStock: Pacific Stock-Design Pics, 15; Thinkstock: kershawj, 6

Design Elements:
Shutterstock: Andrii_M, Limbad, Sara Berdon, yyang

Printed and bound in the USA.
10028S17CG

TABLE OF CONTENTS

CHAPTER 1

A REAL-LIFE DRAGON

Lumbering out of the jungle comes the world's largest lizard. From its rounded snout, it flicks its long, forked tongue in and out of its mouth. Its massive body is covered in what looks like armor. Its long, sharp claws look as though they could rip anything apart. It's easy to see how this animal, the Komodo dragon, earned its name.

Komodo dragon

DRAGON MYTH AND REALITY

You've probably read about dragons in storybooks. These dragons fly through the air. They breathe fire. They may stand guard over a maiden in a tower. These dragons are myths.

The Komodo dragon was once thought to be just a myth. Stories of a dragon-like creature living on the island of Komodo in Indonesia spread for many years. Local people called it a "land crocodile." Until about 100 years ago, no outside scientist had actually seen the creature. When one scientist finally saw the huge beasts with his own eyes, he named it Komodo dragon, after the creatures of myth.

CHAPTER 2

SPOTTING A KOMODO DRAGON

The Komodo dragon is a gigantic beast. Its long body stretches up to 10.3 feet (3.1 meters) long. Its tail is huge and muscular. The animal weighs about 154 pounds (70 kilograms). At such a large size, this creature easily overpowers its **prey**.

The Komodo dragon moves its wide, flat head and rounded snout as it checks out its surroundings. A long, forked tongue flicks in and out of its mouth. Its teeth are sharp and **serrated**.

prey—an animal hunted by another animal for food
serrated—having a jagged edge

The largest Komodo dragons weigh up to 366 pounds (166 kg). However, average Komodos weigh less than half that size.

DRAGON FACT

Komodo dragons are rarely spotted in the wild. For scientists to study them, they must set out food to lure the creatures out of hiding.

Rough, bony scales cover the dragon's entire body. This tough, armored skin may be blue, orange, gray, or green. It helps give the Komodo its fearsome appearance.

The creature's bowed legs may make it look clumsy. But this does little to slow the Komodo down. It can sprint up to 13 miles (20 kilometers) per hour. It's as fast as some dogs. Each muscular leg ends in long claws help rip apart the dragon's pre

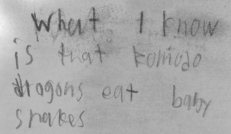

What I know is that komodo dragons eat baby snakes

Dragon Teeth

The Komodo dragon's mouth holds 60 short, razor-sharp teeth. The teeth curve inward. This helps it tear into prey. Komodos go through many sets of teeth. A Komodo dragon may go through four or five sets of teeth in its lifetime.

A BEAST AMONG LIZARDS

Komodo dragons are lizards. Lizards are a type of reptile. All reptiles have dry, scaly skin. Scientists further divide lizards into groups. Komodo dragons are a kind of monitor lizard. The **carnivorous** monitors have powerful jaws. Their tails are long and whiplike. Komodo dragons are the largest and heaviest lizards on Earth.

A Komodo dragon's skin is covered in scales.

THE ISLAND GIANTS

How did Komodo dragons become the largest lizards on Earth? One idea is that early relatives of these creatures once lived on a large continent. These early lizards were much smaller. Then they began moving to islands. With more prey and fewer **predators**, the lizards' offspring slowly became larger and larger.

COLD-BLOODED CREATURES

All reptiles are **cold-blooded**. They cannot make their own body heat. Komodo dragons spend lots of time in the sun to keep warm. At night or during rain, they may hide in a lair—an underground **burrow** that keeps them warm.

carnivorous—eating only meat
predator—an animal that hunts another animal for food
cold-blooded—having a body that needs to get heat from its surroundings
burrow—an underground home of an animal

Lizard versus Snake

Lizards are very similar to another reptile—snakes. Both are cold-blooded. Both have scaly skin. However, they differ in important ways. And it's not just the legs! While many lizards have legs, not all do. The key differences are lizards' ears and eyelids. Lizards can't hear as well as humans, but they do have external ear holes. Snakes do not. Snakes do have a scale that protects the eye, but lizards have movable eyelids.

CHAPTER 3

LIVING KOMODO STYLE

Komodo dragons live in only a tiny part of the Earth. Five small islands in Indonesia make up their **range**. Komodo, Rinca, Gili Dasami, Gili Montang, and Flores are home to this animal.

Komodo is the largest of the islands. It is just 150 square miles (241 square km). Two Komodo Islands could fit in New York City!

The land where this lizard roams is rugged and hilly. Parts of the islands are forests with dense plant life. The weather is dry and hot. The islands get little to no rainfall eight months out of the year. During the day it averages 95 degrees Fahrenheit (35 degrees Celsius). Komodos thrive in this heat. Sometimes Komodos trek up the mountains and ridgetops where the air is cooler and moist.

range—an area where an animal mostly lives

a Komodo dragon on Rinca Island, Indonesia

GROUND DWELLERS

Many other lizards live in trees. Komodo dragons dwell on the ground. On the ground they bask in the heat of the sun. They watch for prey in dry grasslands and forests. At night they retreat to their lairs.

A Komodo dragon comes out of its lair.

DRAGON FACT

Volcanoes long ago created the islands where Komodo dragons dwell today. These volcanoes are no longer active.

CHAPTER 4
FIGHTING FOR LAND

Komodo dragons like hanging out alone. Their small lairs are just large enough for one dragon. In the day they roam and hunt alone. While roaming, a dragon stays in a certain area. Each dragon's **territory** depends on its size. An average adult covers about 1.2 square miles (2 square km) every day.

However, this territory does not belong entirely to one Komodo. Territories often overlap. Though they hunt alone, when a Komodo takes down large prey, other dragons will often gather together to feed.

FIGHTING DRAGONS

A dragon's size determines its **dominance** within a territory. Males may fight to prove who is the most powerful. Using their muscular tails as support, male dragons stand tall on their hind legs to attack. With their front legs, the dragons wrestle. They attempt to throw each other to the ground. These attacks are often violent and bloody.

territory—an area of land that an animal claims as its own to live in

dominance—control because of strength or power

Two Komodo dragons fight one another.

CHAPTER 5

EATING LIKE A DRAGON

Komodo dragons are not picky eaters. They will eat just about any animal they find. Larger Komodos hunt deer, water buffalo, and wild boar. Smaller Komodo dragons eat rodents, birds, and eggs. Sometimes they eat smaller lizards—including other Komodos! They **scavenge** for dead animals as well.

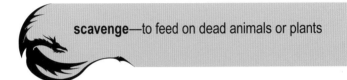

scavenge—to feed on dead animals or plants

water buffalo

TONGUE DETECTIVES

The Komodo dragon picks up scents in the air with its tongue. The tongue can detect prey up to 3.1 miles (5 km) away. The Komodo can tell the direction of an animal based on what side of its tongue picked up a stronger scent. After each flick in and out of its mouth, the Komodo rubs its tongue along the roof of its mouth. Particles from the scent touch special organs. The organs detect even faint traces of a nearby animal's scent.

DRAGON FACT

Though Komodo dragons mainly stay on land, these island dwellers are excellent swimmers. They've been spotted miles from shore, traveling between nearby islands.

WAITING FOR PREY

As hunters, Komodos do not seek out their prey. Rather, after a Komodo has picked up the scent of an approaching animal, it lies in wait. It **camouflages** itself in bushes or tall grass. Then the Komodo patiently waits. When the prey comes near, the dragon pounces. With sharp claws and strong legs, the Komodo grabs hold of its victim. Then it sinks its jagged teeth into the animal's flesh.

Komodo dragons use long, sharp claws to attack their prey.

This Komodo dragon bites its prey—a goat.

Komodo dragons make gaping wounds with their serrated teeth. But the bite also poisons their prey. After an attack the prey may escape, but not for long. Within 24 hours the **venom** will spread. Untroubled by their victim's escape, the Komodo calmly follows its prey. It uses its sharp sense of smell to track the animal for miles, eventually locating the prey, now dead.

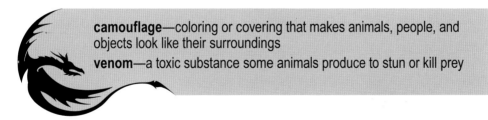

camouflage—coloring or covering that makes animals, people, and objects look like their surroundings

venom—a toxic substance some animals produce to stun or kill prey

DRAGON FACT

Komodo dragons have great eyesight. They can spot prey as far as 985 feet (300 m) away.

TIME TO EAT!

Once their prey is at hand, Komodo dragons eat incredibly quickly. They may eat up to 5.5 pounds (2.5 kg) of meat in a single minute. They have amazing appetites as well. Some Komodos have been known to eat 80 percent of their body weight in a single feeding. Because they eat so much at one time, Komodos don't have to eat very often. Some only eat about once a month.

Komodo dragons gather together to feast on prey.

The dominant Komodo gets to eat first at a kill. Smaller dragons have to wait their turn. They often must pick at whatever remains of the prey. Because Komodo dragons are so solitary in nature, group feedings are one of the few times that males and females are together.

Well fed, the Komodo dragon can relax. It has no predators of its own. There are no predators in their habitat that are bigger or more dangerous than the Komodo. They are at the top of their **food chain**.

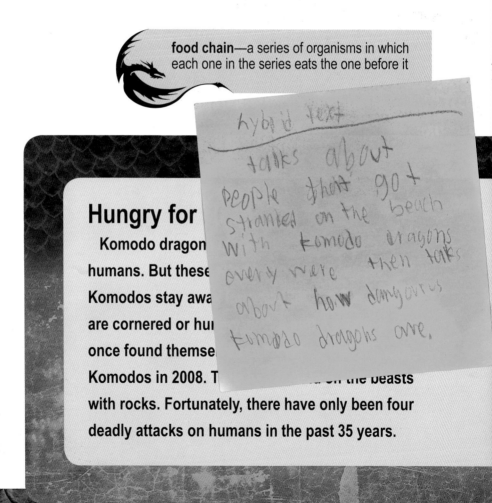

food chain—a series of organisms in which each one in the series eats the one before it

Hungry for

Komodo dragon
humans. But these
Komodos stay awa
are cornered or hu
once found themse
Komodos in 2008. T ...... on the beasts
with rocks. Fortunately, there have only been four
deadly attacks on humans in the past 35 years.

hybrid text

talks about people that got stranded on the beach with komodo dragons every were then talks about how dangrous komodo dragons are,

CHAPTER 6

KOMODO DRAGON LIFE CYCLE

Komodo dragons usually **mate** between the months of May and August. Some females do not mate every year. Other females do not mate at all. That's because they can lay eggs without mating with a male. This happens when this solitary creature moves to an area without any males. The female will lay eggs from which only male Komodo dragons hatch. She can then mate with the male offspring and begin a new population of Komodo dragons.

Females that have mated lay their eggs in September, after the hottest months have passed. They may lay up to 30 soft, white-shelled eggs. Then they cover them with dirt and leaves.

Komodo dragons bury their eggs in underground nests.

The Komodo mother does not stray far from her nest. She may even build decoy nests. The decoys confuse predators that might steal the eggs. She keeps watch, **incubating** the eggs. They will incubate for up to nine months. Once they have hatched, though, the mother's work is done. Young Komodos fend for themselves as soon as they hatch.

mate—to join together to produce young
incubate—to keep eggs at a suitable temperature while they develop

Stealing Nests

Sometimes a mother Komodo will build her own nest for her eggs. But she prefers a nest already built. The orange-footed scrubfowl nests from January to April. So its nest is abandoned by the time the Komodo is ready to lay eggs. The leaves and debris that make up the nest are a natural incubator.

GROWING UP DRAGON

Newly hatched Komodo dragons are about 12 inches (30 centimeters) long. They weigh about 3.5 ounces (100 grams). Almost immediately after hatching, the baby dragons run away from the nest. They race to the top of a nearby tree. They must avoid being eaten by their mother or other Komodos!

These Komodo dragon hatchlings are emerging from eggs in their underground nest.

young Komodo dragon, about 4 days old

For another eight months, the young dragons live in trees. They grow large, eating bugs, eggs, small lizards, and birds. As they grow, they also change color. Greenish in color when they hatch, they become gray or reddish-brown as they age.

The larger they get, the more time Komodo dragons will spend on the ground. But younger dragons still face danger below. Although adult Komodos have no predators, young dragons do. Large snakes, wild boars, and other animals may prey on them.

By the time they are 4 years old, young Komodos are about 4 feet (1.2 m) long. They have grown large enough to leave the safety of the trees and live on the ground. Komodo dragons reach adulthood at about 9 or 10 years old. They can expect a long life for a lizard. In the wild Komodos may live up to 30 years.

CHAPTER 7

DRAGONS IN DANGER

Without any predators, it may seem like the Komodo dragon is safe from any threat. But there are only about 3,000 Komodo dragons living in the wild. Only about 600 of those are females capable of laying eggs. With these low numbers, the fate of this animal is in question.

THREATS TO DRAGONS

One threat facing this animal is the destruction of their homes. As people cut through land, they tear down the plants that the Komodo uses to camouflage itself. The animal population dwindles as humans hunt both Komodos and their prey. With a limited food source, Komodos have more difficulty finding their next meals.

As their food sources decline, some Komodos resort to eating livestock. When this happens, some farmers see the Komodos as pests. To protect their livestock, some farmers bait the Komodos with poisoned meat, killing them.

The Komodo dragon is considered vulnerable. This means it's not yet **endangered**, but could be soon.

Locals trap a Komodo dragon.

endangered—at risk of dying out

HOPE FOR DRAGONS

Today most Komodos live in protected areas. Komodo National Park opened in 1980 in Indonesia. The park protects Komodo dragons and other wildlife. Scientists at zoos have worked to breed Komodos. Some of these Komodos may be released into the wild. Strict laws against **poaching** help protect this lizard. As more people take an interest in the fate of these rare dragons, their futures may be saved. Komodo dragons are not myths. It is up to us to prevent the last of our real-life dragons from disappearing.

Children look at a Komodo dragon at the Houston Zoo.

You Can Help Too

You may not live near any Komodo dragons, but your actions impact the wildlife around you. The choices you make can help all creatures survive for years to come. Don't litter or dump waste. Plant **native** trees and shrubs when others are cut down. Go to your local library. Learn about the wildlife in your area and how you can help protect it. Your actions may seem small, but they can help in big ways.

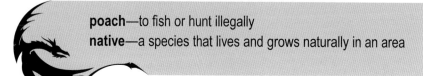

poach—to fish or hunt illegally
native—a species that lives and grows naturally in an area

KOMODO DRAGON FACTS

EYE

SNOUT

TONGUE

SCALES

CLAW

TAIL

COMMON NAME:

Komodo dragon, also called the Komodo monitor;
called *ora* (land crocodile) by people of Komodo Island

SCIENTIFIC NAME:

Varanus komodoensis

RANGE:

Indonesia's Lesser Sunda Islands (Komodo, Rinca,
Gili Montang, Gili Dasami, and Flores)

HABITAT:

tropical savanna forests, beaches, and ridgetops

SIZE:

up to 10.3 feet (3.1 m) long; can weight up to 366 pounds
(166 kg); average weight is about 154 pounds (70 kg)

COLOR:

Adults are typically brown, green, or gray and can have
hues of black, blue, orange, red, or yellow. Young are
green with black and yellow markings. Tongues normally
are yellow.

NATURAL PREDATORS:

PREY:

large prey, such as large water buffalo, deer, carrion,
and pigs

LIFE SPAN:

30 years

GLOSSARY

burrow (BUHR-oh)—an underground home of an animal

camouflage (KA-muh-flahzh)—coloring or covering that makes animals, people, and objects look like their surroundings

carnivorous (kahr-NI-vuh-ruhss)—eating only meat

cold-blooded (KOHLD-BLUHD-id)—having a body that needs to get heat from its surroundings

dominance (DAH-muh-nanss)—control because of strength or power

endangered (in-DAYN-juhrd)—at risk of dying out

food chain (FOOD CHAYN)—a series of organisms in which each one in the series eats the one before it

incubate (INK-yoo-bate)—to keep eggs at a suitable temperature while they develop

mate (MATE)—to join together to produce young

native (NAY-tuhv)—a species that lives and grows naturally in an area

poach (POHCH)—to fish or hunt illegally

predator (PRED-uh-tur)—an animal that hunts another animal for food

prey (PRAY)—an animal hunted by another animal for food

range (RAYNJ)—an area where an animal mostly lives

scavenge (SKAV-uhnj)—to feed on dead animals or plants

serrated (SER-ay-tid)—having a jagged edge

territory (TER-uh-tor-ee)—an area of land that an animal claims as its own to live in

venom (VEN-uhm)—a toxic substance some animals produce to stun or kill prey

READ MORE

Ganeri, Anita. *The Story of the Komodo Dragon*. Fabulous Animals. Chicago: Raintree, 2016.

Hirsch, Rebecca E. *Komodo Dragons: Deadly Hunting Reptiles*. Comparing Animal Traits. Minneapolis: Lerner Publishing, 2015.

Pope, Kristen. *On the Hunt with Komodo Dragons*. On the Hunt with Animal Predators. Mankato, Minn.: Child's World, 2016.

INTERNET SITES

FactHound offers a safe, fun way to find Internet sites related to this book. All of the sites on FactHound have been researched by our staff.

Here's all you do:

Visit *www.facthound.com*

Type in this code: 9781515750697

 Check out projects, games and lots more at **www.capstonekids.com**

CRITICAL THINKING USING THE COMMON CORE

1. Where does the Komodo dragon live? Name two features about where it lives. (Key Idea and Details)

2. Reread the Dragon Fact on page 25. Use a dictionary to define the word *vulnerable*. (Craft and Structure)

3. Name one body part that helps the Komodo dragon hunt. What if it did not have this body part? How might it hunt differently? (Integration of Knowledge and Ideas)

INDEX